The activities

- The activities in this book are designed to show whether your children are 'ready' to read or are ready for a more difficult reading level. Their wish to read is the best sign of readiness.
- Many skills are involved, but most of them will be mastered unconsciously, just as your children learned to talk without direct teaching. They do not have to be equally good at, for instance, seeing letters distinctly, drawing, copying or telling a story. Success in particular activities should help you to find their strong points.
- The chart on page 32 details some of the skills and the ways these are linked with progress in learning to read.

The stories at Level 2

- These stories are fuller and a little more complex than those at Level 1. They introduce a greater number of characters, including all the residents of West Street. The words are repeated less frequently and the sentences are longer. At this level you should begin to emphasise the child's independent reading more.
- Before you start reading with your children, read the story and activities first yourself, so that you become familiar with the text and the best way to give it expression and emphasis when reading it aloud.
- Always sit comfortably with your child, so that both of you can see the book easily.
- Read the story to your child, making it sound as interesting as possible. Add comments on the story and the pictures if you wi... ...ge your child ... the ... and to ... nd ... ng, ... d that ... with. Encourage ... ild to take the book away and to look through it alone.
- Next time you look at the book with your child, suggest "Let's read the story together. You join in with me." The text in the speech bubbles is often the same as the text at the bottom of the page, so one of you can read the text in the bubbles, and one can read the text at the bottom of the page. This time encourage your child to guess words from the context. Follow the words with your finger under them as you read. Don't stop to repeat words; keep the interest up and the story line flowing along.
- Now ask your child, "Do you want to read the story to me this time?" If your child would like to do this, join in where necessary if help is needed.

The activities at Level 2

- The activities at the back of the book need not be completed at once. They are not a test, but will help your child to remember the words and stories and to develop further skills required for becoming a fluent reader.

The activities are often divided into three parts.

- One part is designed to encourage you

both to talk about the stories, and to link them where possible with your child's own experiences. Encourage your child to predict what will happen and to recall the main events of the story. Change the wording of the story as much as you like and encourage your children to tell you about the story in their own way.

- One part encourages children to look back through the book to find general or specific things in the text or the pictures. Your child learns to begin to look at the text itself, and to recognise individual words and letters more precisely. The activities state clearly when you should give a letter its name, and when you should sound it out. The activities also introduce more writing, largely copying from words in the original story. If your children find this too difficult, copy the words onto a piece of paper for them to trace over.
- One part suggests drawing or writing activities which will help your children feel they are contributing actively to the story in the book.
- When you and your child have finished all the activities, read the story together again before you move on to another book. Your child should now feel secure with it and enjoy being able to read the story to you.

A horse for Liz

by Helen Arnold

Illustrated by Tony Kenyon

A Piccolo Original
In association with Macmillan Education

Liz was reading a book.
It was a book about horses.

Tamla had a toy horse.
But Liz wanted a real horse.

I can ride my horse in a race.

I won the race.

I can jump over the fence.

I can ride across the sky.

I can ride over the sea.

I can ride with the cowboys.

I can ride across the desert.

I can ride in the parade.

I can ride in the circus.

Wake up, Liz.
It's time for tea.

Things to talk about with your children

1. Liz dreamed about a lot of different horses, didn't she?
How many horses did she ride?
Which of them would you like to ride?

2. Do you like reading books about horses? Do you read books about other animals?
Which animals do you like best?

Looking at pictures and words with your children

1. Which horse jumped into the sky?
   Can you find a picture of it?

   Which horse rode across the desert?
   Can you find a picture of it?

2. The word **ride** begins with the sound **r**

   Can you find all the words in the story that begin with the sound **r**

   How many times can you find the word **ride** in the story?

3. I'll read these bits of the story out to you. Can you tell me what words I've missed out?

I can ride ________ the sky. I can ride ________ the parade.

I can ride ________ the sea.

4. Here is a sentence from the story. Let's read it together. Something funny has happened to some of the words – they've been printed back to front! Can you point to the words which are written back to front? (Make sure you read the words aloud correctly.)

I can edir my esroh in a ecar

Would you like to try writing the words the right way round?

Things for your child to do

1. Choose a picture you like in the story. Look at it very carefully. Now give me the picture. Can you tell me everything you can remember that is in the picture?

Now we'll change over. I'll choose a picture and tell you everything I can remember about it. Can you find the picture and tell me anything I have forgotten?

2. Can you draw a picture of Liz on her horse?

These activities and skills:	will help your children to:
Looking and remembering	hold a story in their heads, retell it in their own words.
Listening, being able to tell the difference between sounds	remember sounds in words and link spoken words with the words they see in print.
Naming things and using different words to explain or retell events	recognise different words in print, build their vocabulary and guess at the meaning of words.
Matching, seeing patterns, similarities and differences	recognise letters, see patterns within words, use the patterns to read 'new' words and split long words into syllables.
Knowing the grammatical patterns of spoken language	guess the word-order in reading.
Anticipating what is likely to happen next in a story	guess what the next sentence or event is likely to be about.
Colouring, getting control of pencils and pens, copying and spelling	produce their own writing, which will help them to understand the way English is written.
Understanding new experiences by linking them to what they already know	read with understanding and think about what they have read.
Understanding their own feelings and those of others	enjoy and respond to stories and identify with the characters.

First published 1990 by Pan Books Ltd,
Cavaye Place, London SW10 9PG

9 8 7 6 5 4 3 2 1

Editorial consultant: Donna Bailey

British Library Cataloguing in Publication Data
Arnold, Helen
A horse for Liz.
1. English language. Readers — For children
I. Title II. Series
428.6
ISBN 0–330–30698–7

Printed in Hong Kong